Creative Caring

in appreciation
for being so
caring

Jean Kitzinger

&

Creative Caring

Support & encouragement ideas
to help others through life's challenges

☞

Beth Kitzinger & Linda Davies Rockey

SUPPORT PUBLICATIONS / EAST LANSING, MICHIGAN

Copyright © 1995 by Beth Kitzinger and Linda Davies Rockey

Publisher's Cataloging-in-Publication Data
Kitzinger, Beth
Creative Caring: support & encouragement ideas to help others through life's challenges
p.   cm.

ISBN 0-9646115-0-3
1.Helping Behavior. 2.Caring. 3.Encouragement. I. Rockey, Linda Davies, II. Title.
BF637.H4H83   1995   158.25—dc20   95-68237

PUBLISHERS DESIGN SERVICE
Project Coordination: Alex Moore
Cover Design: Debra Anton
Text Design: Mary Jo Zazueta

Printed in the United States of America
First Edition: June 1995

10 9 8 7 6 5 4 3 2 1

*This book is dedicated with love and understanding
to our children,
who we hope will always be ready and willing
to offer support to those in need.*

CONTENTS

PREFACE

*T*he inscription on a card that one of us sent the other read, "Friendship is a delicate combination of admiration, trust, empathy, two forks and one dessert."

As best friends for the past fifteen years, we have had many opportunities to listen, offer advice, share tears and enjoy many chocolate desserts! We always take the time to support and encourage each other by leaving a casserole, sending flowers, always being available to listen...

Knowing how important this has been to us, we hope that you will use our ideas to reach out and support someone you know.

CB

Illness

If someone you know is hospitalized or home ill, support their immediate family by organizing coworkers, friends or neighbors to bring dinner in nightly.

*F*or a friend suffering from a chronic illness, make a contribution to the medical group that sponsors research toward a cure. Acknowledge that you've done this in a card to them.

When a friend is going for extensive tests, ask if they are going alone and if so, accompany them if you can.

Take a few minutes to call someone who has been ill and <u>just listen.</u>

When someone in your office is
seriously ill and must be off work for an
extended time, get together with your
coworkers and donate some of your paid
vacation days to them.

After a hospital stay, welcome your friend home with balloons and banners.

*O*rganize a "pack-the-freezer" effort for someone with a family member who is hospitalized for a lengthy time. Don't forget to make a schedule of who will bring the perishables once per week to use with the frozen meals.

Call a school and ask for a class to draw pictures to cheer up someone who is seriously ill.

As holidays approach, offer to help with cards and shopping, picking up items that the family might need such as Halloween costumes or Easter candy.

When a serious illness occurs, organize a fund-raiser to help defer expenses.

Arrange to care for a hospitalized person's pet, so that this will be one less worry for them.

Take a cassette tape player with headphones and some relaxation tapes along for your friend going into the hospital for tests. This will help ease their anxiety and help pass the time.

When someone is ill, they may not be getting support from their family. Take the initiative and do something for them. Examples are cleaning, shopping or returning phone calls.

If someone must travel to get special medical help, such as going to the Mayo Clinic, call ahead and arrange for a dinner gift certificate to be waiting at their hotel so they know you're thinking of them.

Rent two movies, one funny and one
sad. Then take the time to watch them
with your friend. Sometimes this is the
best way to allow the tears to fall.

If the ill person has children, offer to take them for a few hours.

A gift of stationery or cards is wonderful
to occupy one's time.

P*ick up a craft item or a book they would be interested in.*

*T*ake nail polish, combs and brushes to a friend's, then give her a manicure and fix her hair.

*L*ift your bedridden friend's spirits by helping him shave, comb his hair, and splash on some favorite after-shave.

*P*ick up and return library books or videos for your friend.

If someone is going through physical therapy, offer to drive them once a week and assist with the therapy if needed.

Call a friend and say you're bringing over dinner tonight (include candles if you have them.) It is always a good idea to ask what the person can eat and if there is something they'd really like.

Telephone your friend and say you're going shopping. Ask if she'd like to go along, if not, ask what you can pick up for her.

If you know someone with a serious illness in the family, offer to make phone calls to family, friends, and coworkers.

If you know someone too ill to read,

rent some books on tapes for them.

If someone you know is having eye surgery, send a bouquet that they can "see" of fragrant flowers such as gardenias.

*T*ake your bedridden friend "out to the movies" by renting a video and making the popcorn to go with it.

If someone you know is too ill to attend their child's play, recital or sports event, attend for them and take pictures or a video for them to see later.

*S*end an ill child a walking balloon
from a local florist. Have the walking
balloon hold a bouquet of other balloons.

Bring a cuddly stuffed animal with a bandage over the part of the animal's body where the child hurts.

*T*ake quiet, yet fun bedside toys and projects to an ill child that will help pass time: a magnetic drawing board, activity books, or hand-held games.

A little cassette player with headphones and a selection of tapes will help a child pass time. Movie soundtracks are especially popular with children.

For a child having surgery, organize a "quiet" party a few days after they return home so that their friends will know the child is recovering.

☙

Divorce

Make an appointment with a lawyer for an hour of consultation for your friend. The first step is the hardest.

*T*reat your friend to a haircut with a
gift certificate from her favorite salon.

Be there when they need to talk about their feelings.

Remember your friend on Valentine's Day with a gift or a card.

Offer to assist on tough days such as court appearances.

Get together with your friend for the three "c's:" coffee, conversation, and chocolate!

If you have time, schedule a walk with your friend on a regular basis, or take an exercise class together.

Ask about holiday plans, they definitely will be different now.

Give your friend a copy of The Good Divorce *book, by Constance R. Ahrons, Ph.D.*

*S*end cope/encouragement cards once a week or write your own words.

*R*ent "Sleepless in Seattle" and watch it together. Better yet, buy your friend a copy.

If you have children, let your friend baby-sit. Not only will she feel needed, but being with children allows one to look past today and into the future.

Give her a catalog of classes at a community college. If possible, take a class with her.

*W*hen the divorce is "final," go with
your friend to the court appearance. Go
out afterwards to celebrate a new
beginning.

New Baby
& Adoption

When visiting the new family, bring something to give the older sibling(s) and give it to them first. A great gift is something they can do quietly and by themselves: workbooks, videotapes, or cassette tapes with a read-a-long book.

*O*ffer to take the older sibling(s) away
for part of the day; to the park, to a
movie, out for lunch. The older child
needs the "break" from the new family
member. This time with a friend will
make the child feel special.

Bring the new mom a gift such as a basket that you can put together yourself with magazines, special coffee or tea, her favorite bath fragrance, and fat-free brownies.

Call your friend with a new baby to tell her you're coming over to watch the baby while she takes a nap, and insist she do it!

If you're a good friend or family member visiting the new family, just start doing the obvious things that need to be done: fold a basket of laundry, pick up the newspapers or put the dishes in the dishwasher.

Offer to let Mom take a shower while you're there, with the peace and security that someone is caring for the baby.

*T*ell the new parent to leave their
laundry outside the door. Pick it up and
return it, clean and folded, to the doorstop
later that day.

*A*s the weeks pass and the visitors fade, bring "take out" lunch from a restaurant and stay and eat it with the new mom.

If the baby is giving mom lots of trouble and frustration (let's face it, all babies do this on some days,) send her a cope or encouragement card from the baby.

*C*all the new mom as often as you can.
If she asks for advice and you've been
there yourself, freely give it. If she
doesn't, just listen.

If you know the baby is really "testing" the mother's patience, send a bouquet of flowers from the baby to her. This is sure to bring a smile to Mom's face, even if it's for the one minute until the baby starts screaming again!

Take the parents-to-be a little stuffed animal with a wind-up music box before the baby is born. Wrap it up and tell them to open it at the hospital. They will be able to find their baby in the nursery by looking for the special stuffed animal.

If your friend is "blessed" with a colicky baby, take over for an hour and let her get outside for fresh air, exercise or to go for a drive.

Think of things to help the mother with a colicky baby ease the isolation, as they really can't leave the house during this period. Visit them frequently and bring lunch in.

A great gift for all children is a
Christmas ornament each year. When
they grow up they will have their own
collection, plus wonderful memories of
their past Christmases.

Give a storage box to new parents to put mementos in. Examples: first pair of baby shoes, a baby outfit, a Halloween costume, report cards, special poems they have written and artwork they make.

Welcome the adopted child with a
balloon bouquet.

Buy the parents of a newly adopted child a baby book to record the life events of their child.

Give the parents a journal to write down
their thoughts and feelings about the
adoption to pass on later to the child.

Help the family to record the special day by giving them a gift certificate for a photo sitting.

Career Changes

If your friend is looking for a new job, buy them time with a resume service company--top it off with envelopes and stamps to get those cover letters and resumes out.

Utilize your own network to assist with other employment opportunities if you can.

Be on the lookout for job ads in newspapers, trade journals or on bulletin boards for someone seeking employment.

Give your friend who is changing jobs or going back to work a basket with lipsticks, perfume and nylons.

*S*end a small bouquet of flowers to your friend starting a new job. It will brighten their desk and help ease first day jitters.

*T*ake a new employee out to lunch on their first day to make them feel welcome. Include their coworkers.

G*ive your friend a "check-up" call to see how things are going with their new job.*

Acknowledge a job change or promotion with flowers, balloons, dinner, new briefcase, or a technical magazine subscription.

If you know someone who has just taken a family leave of absence from their job, give them an appropriate "stay at home" gift such as special cookie sheets, a cookie recipe and the ingredients. Send along a set of children's play bake ware.

*F*or someone who has just gone back to work, give a restaurant gift certificate or even a casserole for the freezer for those "busy days."

Discuss how their life is going to change with the new job and offer support by taking on some responsibilities such as running errands or helping with the children.

*S*chedule a massage to help de-stress
them.

CB

Loneliness

*O*rganize a letter writing campaign. Assign friends or family to send a note on certain days of the week, so that someone living alone can get something in their mail each day.

Send someone lonely a box of gifts for the week. Wrap seven items such as pictures your children have made, a magazine, an envelope of hot chocolate, gum, etc. Send a note along saying to open one per day!

If you know a lonely senior citizen who could use companionship, help that person find a support group or hobby. Go with them the first time.

Offer to take your friend to a movie, bowling, or golfing.

*H*ave a child record a story, sing a song, or recite a poem on a cassette tape and give to a lonely friend.

*F*or someone who can't get out, make video tapes for them. Tape your children, the outdoors, someplace you've visited. It's okay to be silly while making this movie.

*T*ake a cuddly stuffed animal to comfort someone who is lonely.

Organize a progressive dinner once a month for a group of lonely people.

Arrange a surprise visit from a special friend or relative for someone who is lonely.

Leave friendly, caring messages on your friend's answering machine.

Pick up information on community needs and give it to someone you know who has time on their hands.

G*o visit someone lonely and just give them a hug, no other communication is needed!*

When you stop to visit someone who is lonely, stay long enough to let <u>them</u> talk. Lonely people miss talking to others.

Help your friend get involved with children. Daycare centers and preschools always have need for an extra set of loving hands.

Get up early and pick up someone who is lonely. Go someplace and watch the sun come up and share a thermos of coffee.

Remember at the holidays to involve children and senior citizens in local community activities such as helping serve a Thanksgiving meal to the needy and filling Christmas baskets at a local church.

Offer to help your lonely friend find a church that will offer them support and friendship.

When you go to the store to get a card for someone lonely, if you find three or four that are cheery, buy them all and send them on the same day!! Besides the warm words, they'll have the thrill of having their mailbox spilling over!

☙

Moving

A lost tradition is taking some freshly baked cookies, a casserole, or other homemade goodie to a new neighbor moving in to make them feel welcome. So if you have a new neighbor, restart the tradition!

*G*ive a subscription to a local city
events magazine to someone who is new
to the area.

*I*f someone you know is moving, offer to go out collecting boxes for them. Ask if they're ready for help to start putting items in them.

If you are the "handy" type, offer to help put up pictures, light fixtures, or other small changes they need to make.

For someone that is moving, buy gift certificates to hardware stores or general merchandise stores. There are always those unexpected items that you need when setting up a household.

*P*urchase a housecleaning service for either cleaning up their old house or the new one.

If someone you know has moved to your area, help them get acquainted by taking them on a tour and showing them the obvious places they will need to go: grocery stores, banks, the library.

*H*elp them get established by making a
list of your doctors.   Call ahead for
them to ensure that the practice will
accept them.

Give a gift certificate to your favorite restaurant for them to try out.

*I*f they have children, offer to take them while they go out; they won't know who to ask to baby-sit yet.

*P*repare a list of baby-sitters with their names, addresses and ages that you think will work well for their children.

*H*elp them find child care for their
young children. Recommend schools for
their school-age children. Put together a
list of music teachers or coaches to help
get the children back on track with their
activities.

Loss

If someone you know is struggling with a loss, recommend a good counselor to them. If you can, buy their first session and make the appointment. This is particularly important for people who struggle taking the first step.

*D*iscuss the holiday plans.   *Doing what has been traditional may no longer be appropriate.*

Help those coping with a loss to talk about the loved one. Begin the conversation for them about something special you remember.

Offer a shoulder to cry on, for as long as they need it.

Help someone who has lost someone special to start or support a cause that would be meaningful. Examples: A cure for the illness or new safety measures to prevent other accidents.

At holidays or anniversary dates, include the memory of a loved one by getting out pictures, showing a video, making that person's favorite dinner or dessert.

*F*ind out when there are grief seminars
and send the schedule to someone
mourning the loss of a loved one.

*T*ake up a collection from coworkers, friends or neighbors and send a catered dinner to the family. Make sure to call them and ask what the best time for this would be and how many friends and relatives are there.

Holidays are very difficult after you have lost a loved one. Send a card or note to let them know you're thinking about them.

Be patient with people mourning a loss. Help them communicate their feelings to a friend, a minister, or a counselor.

*I*f someone you know has recently lost a child, take them to a "Compassionate Friends" meeting. There are support groups to fit everyone's need.

*O*n special occasions, buy a bouquet of
daisies and take your grieving friend to
the cemetery to place these on the grave
site in memory.   Put your arm around
them in comfort and silence.

Supporting Yourself

*P*ut a daily inspirational reading book by your bedside and read it!! There is a whole section of these in the bookstore. Our favorite is Grace Notes by Alexandra Stoddard.

Go ahead and buy that special coffee or
tea that you like so much.

*T*reat yourself to an occasional bouquet of
flowers. They are reasonably priced these
days and you deserve it.

*L*ock the bathroom door and indulge in a hot bath.

*S*ign up for that class you've been thinking about for years.

*T*ake ten minutes a day to keep a
journal or diary, writing can be very
therapeutic.

D*o something physical, for the stress release as well as to keep in shape.*

Get a pair of extra soft pajamas, the kind that give you a hug.

*E*stablish a weekly ritual of doing
something just for you. Example: Go out
for breakfast by yourself every Tuesday
morning. Pick up your favorite
newspaper on the way. Read, relax, and
collect your thoughts.

*A*t holiday time, remember someone
special that you've lost by making a
contribution to their favorite charity.

*T*ake the time to develop and keep a
best friend relationship.

If you would like further information
regarding quantity discounts or how this
book can be used for your organization's
fundraiser, please contact us at:

Support Publications
P.O. Box 4900
East Lansing, MI 48826